Ella and Anna Learn About Worship

Ella and Anna Learn About Worship

Copyright ©2024, Ashley Wentzel
www.renewedmindbreakthroughs.com
info@renewedmindbreakthroughs.com

Published by Renewed Mind Breakthroughs

Edited by: Ruth Webster

Author Picture: Amanda Rae Linas Photography

ISBN: 979-8-9910849-0-1

Tiegreen, C. (2015). Psalm 136:1. In Dancing in the Desert Devotional Bible (pp. 634). essay, Tyndale House Publishers, Inc. .

Give thanks to the Lord, for He is good. His faithful love endures forever.
Psalm 136:1 NLT

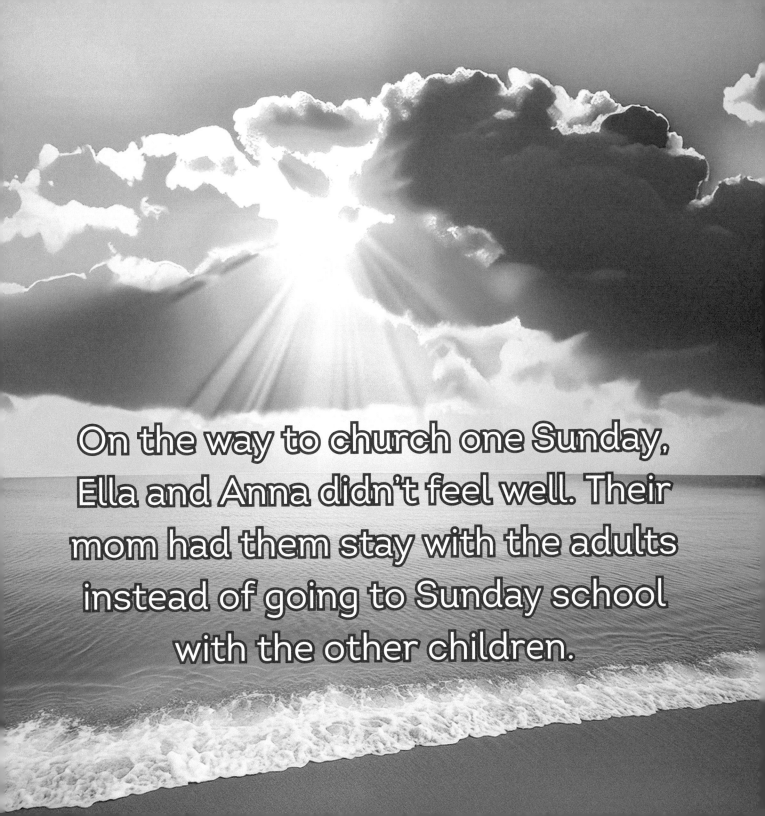

On the way to church one Sunday, Ella and Anna didn't feel well. Their mom had them stay with the adults instead of going to Sunday school with the other children.

After church, Ella asked her mom why she raised her hands during the music. Mom said, "I was worshipping God."

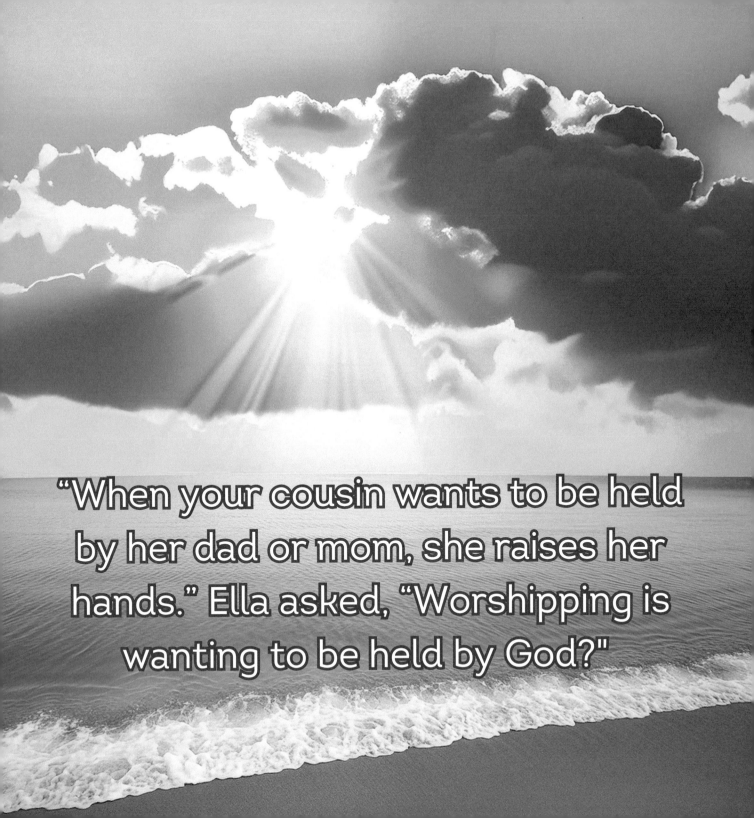

"When your cousin wants to be held by her dad or mom, she raises her hands." Ella asked, "Worshipping is wanting to be held by God?"

Ella's mom explains, "Not exactly; it's making our love for God known! It shows that in our hearts, we are so thankful for all God is and all He has done. However, there is so much more to worship than that. Let's ask the worship leader, David."

"David, may I ask you a question?" Ella continues, "I saw my mom worshipping today, and she explained worship to me, but she thought we should ask you."

David responds, "Jesus told the woman at the well in John 4:23 that true worshippers will worship the Father in spirit and truth, for the Father is seeking such people to worship Him. You see, worship isn't about music. Spirit and truth mean that we know Jesus and His goodness. That we love Him above every person, toy, gift, or ice cream."

"We show our love to God by talking to Him. When we speak to God, it's called praying. We can also dance, sing, or shout for joy, called praise. We can worship God by doing good things for others, which makes God happy. It also pleases God when we give something special to someone in need." "I understand worship more now." Ella thanked David for telling them so much about worship.

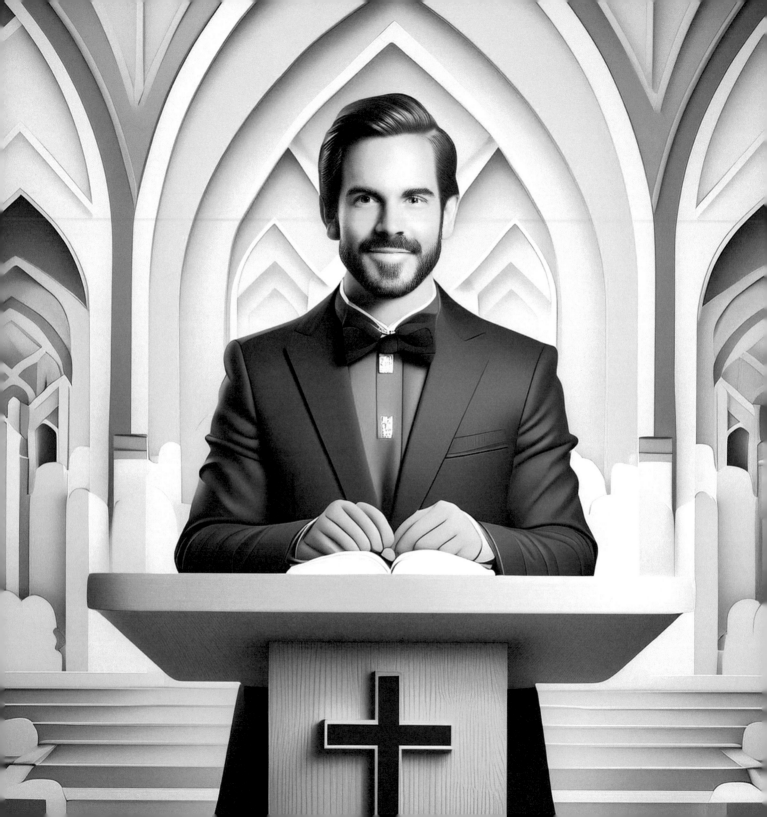

Ella told her mom she still had more questions and wanted to ask Pastor Tom. "Pastor Tom, may I ask you what it means to worship? David talked about worshipping in the spirit, but I don't understand what that means."

Pastor Tom opens the Bible: "Romans 12 says that spiritual worship is offering our bodies as living sacrifices, holy and acceptable to God. Have you learned in Sunday school that before Jesus came to the Earth, people would bring animals to the priests to sacrifice for their sins? A sacrifice is giving up something costly to you. They did this to make up for the things they did wrong."

"When Jesus came, He died as a sacrifice for everyone's sins. By Jesus's death, all our sins have been washed away, and we are forgiven. Jesus then rose from the grave and conquered death. Those who love and believe in Jesus can live with Him forever."

"To be a living sacrifice means we do good out of our love for God. Sometimes, we do this by doing things we don't want, like being honest with our parents when we do something wrong. God also wants us to tell Him when we know we have sinned. This is called repentance. When we speak to God about our sins, ask for forgiveness, and decide not to do it again, or at least try our best not to."

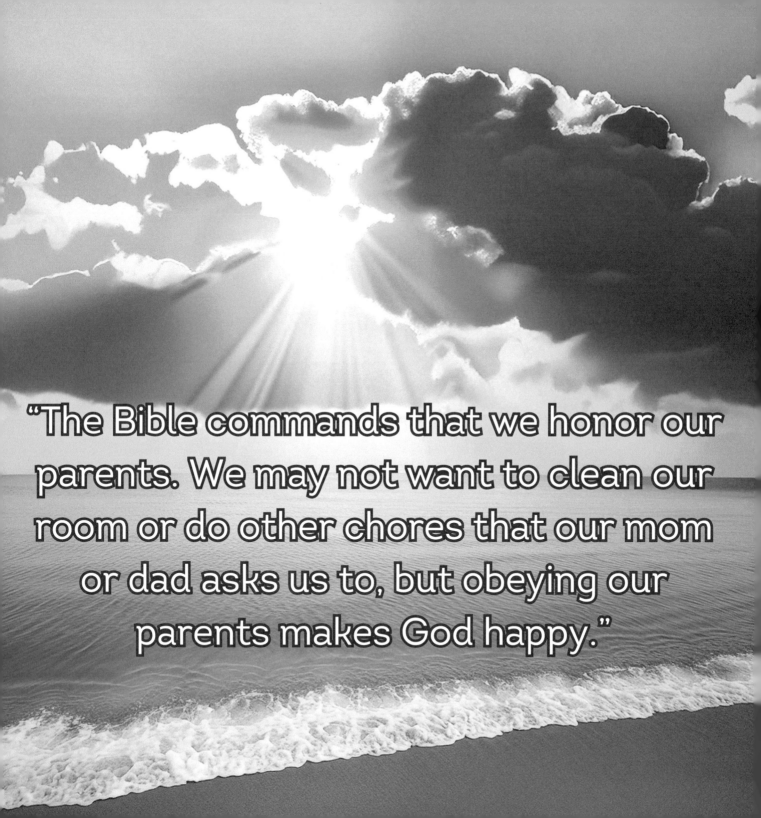

"The Bible commands that we honor our parents. We may not want to clean our room or do other chores that our mom or dad asks us to, but obeying our parents makes God happy."

"It also pleases God when we help someone in need with our time, money, or something else we can give. This is how you can be a living sacrifice, which is spiritual worship." Ella exclaims, "Thank you, Pastor Tom! You have given me a lot to think about."

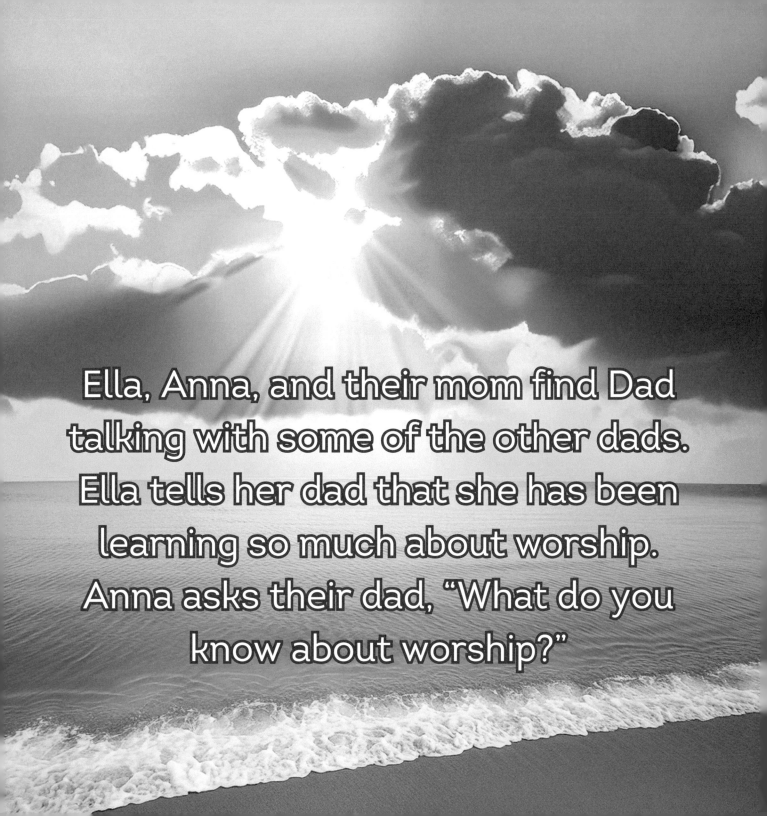

Ella, Anna, and their mom find Dad talking with some of the other dads. Ella tells her dad that she has been learning so much about worship. Anna asks their dad, "What do you know about worship?"

Dad replies, "Jesus tells us in Matthew 15 that worship is from our hearts." Dad pauses and looks at Ella and Anna, "If you say sorry, praise God, or do something good, but it's not out of love; it's not worship. It means nothing to God if it doesn't come from the heart."

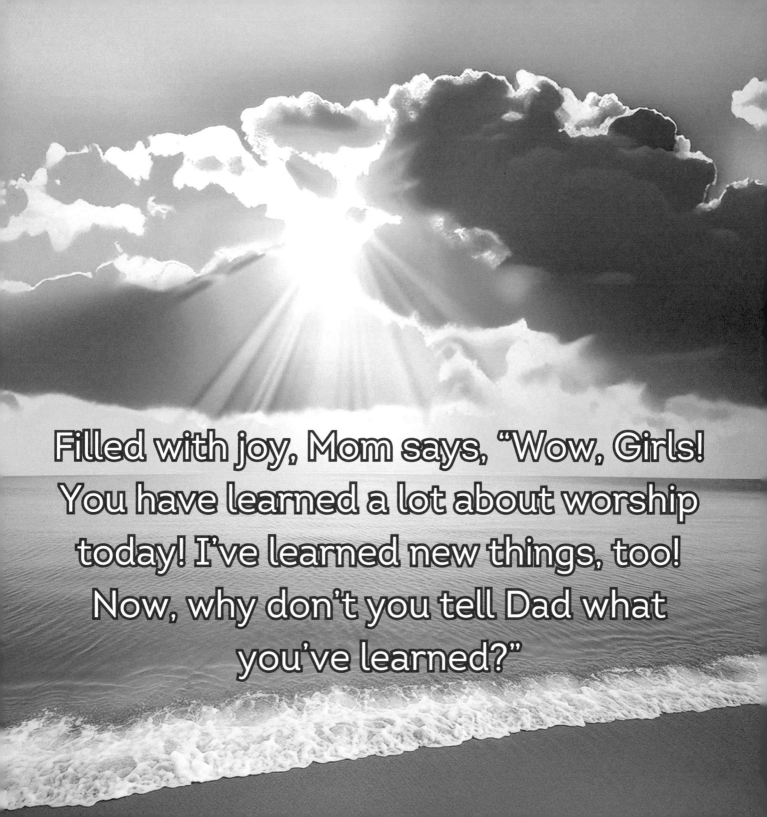

Filled with joy, Mom says, "Wow, Girls! You have learned a lot about worship today! I've learned new things, too! Now, why don't you tell Dad what you've learned?"

Ella replies, "Worship can be many things. Since we love God and Jesus so much, we can dance, sing, and shout about our love, called praise. We can also spend time talking with God, which is called prayer."

Anna adds, "If we sin, we should tell God. If we've wronged a person, we should also tell them. We need to say sorry and mean it with our hearts. Also, when we say sorry, we have to decide not to do it again, which is called repentance."

"Worship can be doing our chores with a cheerful heart. Obeying our parents pleases God. We should also help others who are in need. We can do this by giving some of our birthday money to the kids offering at Sunday school. Then we will be helping someone who needs it, or even someone who is hungry, even though we may want a new toy instead," Ella added.

"That is being a living sacrifice, which is spiritual worship. These things make God happy, and we can show God our love this way," Anna concludes.

Mom exclaims, "You girls are so smart! How are you feeling?" Ella and Anna look at each other, then reply, "Feeling good enough for some ice cream!" Everyone laughs.